Watch

PHOENIX POETS

GREG MILLER

Watch

THE UNIVERSITY OF CHICAGO PRESS

Chicago & London

GREG MILLER is professor of English at Millsaps College. He is the author of a critical study, *George Herbert's "Holy Patterns"* (2007), and of three books of poems, including *Iron Wheel* (1998) and *Rib Cage* (2001), both published in the Phoenix Poets series by the University of Chicago Press.

The University of Chicago Press, Chicago 60637
The University of Chicago Press, Ltd., London
© 2009 by The University of Chicago
All rights reserved. Published 2009
Printed in the United States of America
18 17 16 15 14 13 12 11 10 09   1 2 3 4 5

ISBN-13: 978-0-226-52614-0 (paper)
ISBN-10: 0-226-52614-3 (paper)

Library of Congress Cataloging-in-Publication Data
Miller, Greg, 1957–
    Watch / Greg Miller.
        p. cm. — (Phoenix poets)
    ISBN-13: 978-0-226-52614-0 (pbk. : alk. paper)
    ISBN-10: 0-226-52614-3 (pbk. : alk. paper)
    I. Title. II. Series: Phoenix poets.
    PS3563.I3787W38 2009
    811'.54—dc22   2008047612

CONTENTS

ACKNOWLEDGMENTS

Thanks and acknowledgments are here made to the editors and publications in which some of these poems, sometimes in different versions, first appeared:

Bloodroot: "Salvation" and "Strasbourg"
Ekphrasis: "Holy Conversation"
La Tinaja: "Digs"

"Common Ways" originally appeared in *Image*.

"Wake" was first published in the *Redlands Review* in 2006.

"From the Heights," "Capital Towers," "Protection," "Home," and "The Lotus Tree" first appeared in *Sudan Mississippi* (Birmingham: Mercy Seat Press, 2006).

I am also grateful to the Camargo Foundation in Cassis and the Camac Centre d'Art in Marnay-sur-Seine, France, for residencies in the spring of 2005 and 2007, as well as to Millsaps College in Jackson, Mississippi, for sabbatical and leave time. I am deeply indebted to my friends Michael Wilson and Brian Myers for their patient encouragement, friendship, and advice. I am indebted as well to Dora Robertson, my divisional secretary, for her support over the years.

One

FROM THE HEIGHTS

My vision is partial, my voice middling, and I do not trust myself to
  the heights
though everything here below begins to mingle and seem to me part
  of one canvas:
ego, self-delusion, and pride in an infinite hall of mirrors with
  reflection

mirroring all the old self-deceptions masquerading as penitential
  retractions.
As I ride the bus up the mountain, the water below is no longer
  white as at dawn
when I looked out and felt as if glimpsing the hem of heaven's
  wedding dress.

Earlier even, walking before dawn, I heard one bird singing to itself
  and wondered
to myself whether it was a caged bird on someone's balcony in the
  early cold
till warbling began to answer in another tree across the street and
  then

suddenly a mounting crescendo of other songs loudly greeting the
  morning not yet
arrived, welcoming it into light, into the full presence of day, after
  which I hear
nothing but traffic and the noises that people make going about
  their daily business.

The driver tells me of his town near Spain, north of Toulouse,
   where Louis Treize
tried to kill all the Protestants, where the former president of the
   Spanish Republic
was buried during the civil war because he could find no peace at
   home. (Aragon

and Picasso fled to France, as well, Aragon leaving his mother
   speech to sing
the nightingale's slaughter.) The town still bears the scars of the
   King's bombardments.
We climb higher and higher. I think of Daourt's paintings, of the
   blue openings

that appear so often in them. The labyrinth of scaffolding in one,
   workmen
transfixed in the middle of their labor, and in lonely apartments
   across the way
a woman hidden in impossible contortions, and everywhere sad,
   magisterial cats

looking at us questioningly. Even in her studio, the crossing lines of
   light and shadow,
despite her large, open work space, feels like a spider web of work,
   the rectangular
blue above and the light caught in a high window—glimpses of
   transcendence.

During the occupation, Daourt was protected in the house of the
   Comtesse in Marseille,
but after liberation, her mind grew worse until she began to dress in
   newspapers

and beg in the streets. I climb another hill in Nice to the Chagall
   Museum

where a young Japanese artist asks me (I don't know why) the
   significance
of the "arc-en-ciel" and whether there's a biblical story. I say that
   God destroyed
the world in a flood yet promises never to flood the world again. *It
   means hope.*

In the next room, I stand before *L'Exode*. Christ hangs in the cross
   high in the center
but a flood of people moves up and to the left through fire, a blue
   woman suckling
her child, hopelessly, buildings falling in fire, an artist, head turned
   unnaturally

backward from the window, framed by the cross in the glass (no,
   this is another
painting I'm remembering), a spectral virgin floating toward death,
   a mother and child
born into a sea of floating, drowning faces, and the Christ glowing
   in a white nimbus,

his face dark in contrast. I look back and forth from the slaughter (a
   child put down
on the ground by his mother beside a little billy goat looking up to
   the hand stroking it.)
Christ's right eye is gouged, I think. Then, no: *If thy right eye offend
   thee,*

                                        pluck it out.

DIGS

Marnay-sur-Seine, Champagne

The menhir in a blue field of wheat
cuts a yellow line of rapeseed and the white
lips of recycling pits.

I walk to the darkened holes
of log poles, a long house, Neolithic, the pit
of pottery shards and bone pits, to the dark
hardened place that held fire.
                                        Yesterday
I startled a red fox near the road. It leapt fire
                                        from tuft
            to tuft
into a thicket.
                        I suckle on signs,
a sparrow hawk heckling a heron,
the heron spinning slowly before lifting.

Merovingian graves: a mother and two children
knees to chest in earth *ova*—and I think
much more of me may remain than I had thought or hoped.

On the sarcophagus, white waves, chiseled grain
in wind at an angle, a brass buckle,
an iridescent vial;
                    tumuli, circles in a circle;
an iron age granary;
                    a Roman road.
I imagine angles, eyes, who made what's made,
hands holding stone, bronze, or iron,
or flesh and bone alone, clutches of people,
transfiguring spirits and tongues,
what I speak, eat, and feel made up of bits of them
so grain's good, birth first, and the fresh fruit sweet:
it isn't their ends any more than them I meet.

RIVER

A loon dives in the swollen river.
It followed the river first.
The town lies between it and canals
Diverted from the river.
The beak of the loon is orange,
Its wingspan broader than a duck's.

My father's legs were swollen.
His once thin ankles barely fit his shoes.
His heart no longer fed his body.
Toxins and liquids began to drown him.
His silly doctors didn't see
He couldn't breathe.

My father took me to the river.
We fished for bass and bluegill,
Sunfish, cats. Fat suckers,
Their lips like suction cups,
We put back. Too many little bones
To catch and make you choke.

I no longer want to go fishing.
I don't even want to play
In the water. The boat
Here has no oars, the current
Is too swift. In the dark, teenagers
Discover their body together.

The body feels like a prison.
I kneel by my father's stapled body.
He suctions thick liquid from his lungs.
He coughs to clear them; it hurts.
He wants more air. He wants
To live, the heart's valve's parachutes

Opening with oxygen to feed
The body's healing. A tube
Empties the chest cavity. He excretes
Liquids and poisons.
His shocked kidneys come to life.
His stunned heart beats. His lung

Opens again. He eats. He poops.
He walks. He wants to go home.
On the phone, I catch my sister
Taking him home. It's snowing.
It's cold. My brother and mother
Help him climb the stairs.

I walk down the path
By the shallow canal. I see
A falcon fishing. The power plant
Breathes steam. I hope
The wind won't singe me.
I come to the falls

Where a little dog
Barks and bounces hello. His owner
Smiles and greets me. In the church
Of Saint Laurence I kneel, I
Give thanks, my heart jumps.

EXCESS

after Henri Michaux

I've pushed the door open inside.
I'm here, already, to give you
What you've been needing, what you want

So badly it makes you ache. Take
That sudden illness dropped like lead—
I lift it. I act. My joy's this

Quick. Cuts, stitched, heal, and fever falls.
Hair grows back. Food tastes good.
I stop that superabundance

Of cells. Now only good excess
Greets you with smiles and ease.
You sit in the sun. The carafe

Of water reflects the windows
You can't see, peripheries
Possibilities opening!

You drink them in the sun, happy.
You enjoy the company
Of those you don't know and those

You love, too, here with you.
There is time. Old voices that say
You'll have nothing to offer

I shut them all up.
I show them the door where they will
Be able to cripple only

Themselves with malice. I free you
Too from that malice. You pity them.
You are able to be

Happy in this cool sun.
Slanderers do not
Envy you. (You've done nothing

To merit their anger.) Your conscience is
Light and when able
You've made amends, nor have you

Hidden knives in apologies.
I give you work with a purpose
You've chosen. Anxiety

Doesn't keep you up. When the Black
Ox treads on you his heavy hooves
Don't teach you the wrong things.

(Without him, are we less?)
You welcome love. You grab the lock
Of the child as he comes and don't

Love Chance's ugly butt.
You are not impatient in grief.
Such grief as you meet's a measure

Of love. I wash your future face.
The logjam's broken.
Pleasure flows in again

Through these banks more
Than you thought possible.
I give you this robin's egg blue

Left in the grass to take. I'll say
Hello in the morning. We can meet
Friends and walk if you like.

NOT PROUD

It's easy after the intensity
Of tubes, horns, and doctors to think
Maybe artless misery's what's true.
Arch Emily seemed to think so,
Who liked the look. But I give you the lie,
Death: die, you mere measurer.
You're mean, and at your best if not
A sedan at least you're an easy chair.
We don't know you for what you do but for what
You undo, and what's true you can't undo.

"PAIN'S REQUIRED, SUFFERING OPTIONAL"

Knowing he shouldn't feel so out of sorts,
Anxious in crowds, though crowds take little note
In point of fact, the pain in two small points
In the front of his head, radiating out
Making him dizzy, underwater, caught
Fearfully near the edge (the edge? of what?)
This too shall pass, he's old enough to know,
But to what end, nothing he knows will show.
The middle of the road (more near the end)
With money enough (he can pretend)
Lucky in love in its various forms
Spouse, family, friendship, students (life is sweet)
He needs to find some friend to pull this splinter
Out of his gray matter and make him lighter
Again as (mercifully) he's often been.

GASCOIGNE'S WEEDS

No one has planned
what grows in this ditch:
a couple of wild irises,
dark purple; and lighter
purple thistles whose leaves
imitate white rock; and then
the small, drooping blue flowers
whose leaves and stems are hairy
(I swear) and also
silvery; and wild mustard,
spindlier and higher than the rest,
with pale joints like Tinkertoys.
I'm leaving out the yellow
dandelion and the strange
colorless flowers with black
dots in the center of pale green
cups that the bees love so
that they make bee parties
and get unruly and make a racket.
(I swear, I had to stop
and figure it out!)
I say I saw a rock lizard, too,

flecked black and gray with bits
of what looked like rock
hanging from him.
I looked at him.
He became a rock.
So much seems to aspire

to be dry, white, and rocklike
in the pit of the ditch
and it isn't only
the failure I admire.

WATCH

We pass the straits of the Cape
where grazing whales gather,
though they're not, I'm told, social
creatures by nature.

Alice asks how they can sleep
if they must think to breathe.
Cranial hemispheres wink and wake
and alternate,

so whales are half-awake
and half-asleep, balanced between each
of our states
through dive and breach.

Once on the kitchen wall
of a dune shack I saw,
like a headdress,
the baleen of a whale—

frayed filaments
run from a thin,
curled, rib-like bone:
sieves for the sea.

Like this sickle-moon fin
"negatively buoyant"
I sink in sleep,
but end, I think, where I begin.

Following one as it leaves
two other whales we see
suddenly not what we're heading for
but the asymmetrically

colored snout of a fin whale
as it rises parallel
within a stone's
throw of the boat,

the great eye set back
water crashing rushing
to let me see where it ought to be.
I lose track,

the mottled chin's marble
veined, swirling
through its green veil, which
the top jaw slits.

And then, that's it,
I think. Nights I'm thrown
upright from my rest. Brine
thumps my chest.

CALL

Doves coupled in the limbs outside my room,
and as I write, another grooms her neck.
Companionate, my body's length from me
in the sun, she scratches once behind each eye,
then fans her tail plumes, white at the ends,
and pulls and straightens some. Her eyes are red,
I noticed, when she looked inside to see
if I might give her something, so I thought,
though she seems much more interested in me
as curiosity than anything.

She sounds her call, a hollow wooden bell,
just twice, then flies, her wings whistling a song
to the umbrella pine behind, his voice
percussive like a flare drum, quiet now.

The body that I saw swimming the coast
I lost as I looked down. It swims back now.
Another bell, a tea spoon on a glass
(apartments higher up), the sea below
lapping at the white rock. The swimmer swims
closer to shore. The spoon rings. A door shuts.

SENS

Christ's the dark pistil (five red petals point)
Transecting with golden bars the bass viol,
His consort's honeycomb, in counterpoint
As red moves toward me through my blue denial
Above the abandoned Samaritan,
The fall, the law, as if his sacrifice
Transfuses hives with the honey that ran
Straight from the center like a fragrant spice.
The facing apse: lids pop and people peep,
Full bodied, from graves. They are whole again
Though this window's not: blank-pocked. Devils leap
Down: red, blue (finned?). The loved, in lines, walk in,
Or walk together on the way they know
Will show the way, or this is what they show.

SHINE
after Robinson Jeffers's "The Purse Seine"

Running through a eucalyptus
Stand in the hills—pips, strips
Of bark like flesh trees slough off—

I caught in a manzanita bush's
Red thorns the plump form of a snake
Curled high enough to fend off swipes

A bandit patiently made
At the bush's base to knock it down
Rattling though it didn't quite strike

Yet as I watched them play their life
And death game from my near distance
Transfixed like the snake by stalemate.

In the mid eighties when I would
Drive to those hills at night to watch
Cities across the Bay like purse-

Seines skimming shallows lift grids
Of light they caught without ever
Drawing the luminous fish in

I feared the end of human time
Men of state seemed to think, I thought,
Eternal rhyme could catch if caught.

LOST

A cloud from the Cape's base stalks us catlike
making fantastic shapes rising and stretching,
white megalithic pincers and mute O's,
until the wind turns west again and I'm lost.
I hear the breaking waves, one warbler, then
the drone of an engine scuttling the cliff.

The villa on the hill with Moorish arches,
low-lying, with some visible escapes
down gardens blooming unapproachably
from the cliffs they skirt, reshapes as it takes
a sea's colonial melting memory,
the town's high walls refuge from Saracens
who whisked the bishop from *Les-Saintes-Maries*.

Churchill summered here. Napoleon spent
the night once in a small, freestanding room.
Some nights storm waves pound rock streams like drums
under your feet as if cracking doom knocked
home, white crests feathering the lighthouse eye.

The Celts built in the hills before the Greeks.
(I climbed to their caves to get my new bearings.)
At dusk in the Greek theater I watch
stars pierce the cobalt dome and I hear wings.

WAKE

I

In the wake of the eye, our oak cracks one thick
limb on a pivot, then lifts, about to split.
From the dark we watch the neighbor's pear splay,
wind fling green pecans, wires block the driveway,
one low black wire (alive?) swinging the road.

Water breaches the levies on our
five-inch black-and-white. A woman floats
a plastic crate. The weak die at the airport,
at Charity, on rooftops, attended,
in attics, when our screen goes out, a bullet.

II   IN THE COLISEUM

*"One of my sons is afflicted. 'Where is
my Nana?' he asks me. What can I say
to him?"* he asks me. A stuttering woman
sits by her sister. *"Oh is she drowning!"*
I don't know what I'm doing and I won't.

III

Troops man roadblocks. Hurricane odor (sweet sour):
mold in the playroom, mold in the tiles,
on dolls, toys, clothes, and books. My head, a child's
swing, turns a hinge-song, rain crow, rotted crown.

Mississippi, September 2005

Two

WHITE (I)

A low tree choked with almost white
blooms battened by thin sheathes
of near see-through accordion
green fights its force

that breaks loose, oozing, with delay.
Lengthening days will bring
bees, breezes, and birds to fire fruit
from lit wet wicks.

His kindness like water wears down
stone. All lightness is his.
When the fruits' hours swell and fall
he will be gone.

THE FUTURE QUEEN

I lie awake long after the lights are out.
Late night's oblivion. Nothing at all.
No dogs howling hearing a branch fall—
or a car backfire or a child shout.
I'm blank. The inky dark is just about
all I can make out. (Crickets climb the wall?)
The clock's heart's spinning silver. I'll recall
nothing of what I'm thinking now, no doubt.
What story would I have myself rehearse?
His bragging got me in this fix. I'd spin
gold out of straw? The fox and the hare may be tricked,
but my name's not right. This nightmare could get worse.
Who will I be then and how will I win?
That little man is furiously exact.

REGRET

My little cat has caught
the reedy warbler,
a yellow ball, a gift
laid at my feet.

It is her nature
to bring such things to me.
And heavier than air,
dumb, flying free,

my nature is to know
regret, to bell my keen
light-footed sorrow
while I can.

1983

WHITE (II)

Snow! Snow! The tile roofs are covered.
The ground is covered. And it's still coming down.
Pale stone and stucco
make the white whiter,
the sky, too, bright white.

In the high desert
above the cloud
line, white peaks broke
the white canopy
of the world's bedroom.

Frozen mist aureoled
streetlamps. We two caught
soft in one
another's arms beneath
the uncurtained

window at the back edge
of the pit looked up
at the stars over the peak
clear nights invisible now
nearly unbearable.

SAIL

I walk back near dusk at meadow's edge
seeing a pale arc shimmering
through the tail's jet-black before I know
it's the tom turning strutting haltingly
for his hens on one leg, his neck light
blue blue-green, the plumage of his head
lifting itself white as he turns
trailing his long, red wattle near the ground,
spreading speckled plumage, wings flaring.
Then he makes himself broad, trembling.

IN ARLES

We walk around the Roman amphitheatre.
We see posters for new blood sports.
They're sandblasting
gray stone white. We sit on scaffolding,
then, in the wind, climb
the new medieval turret.

We take pictures of that old wild
man the muddy Rhône
and each other. I dream
of the Delta, New Orleans. We look
at the sculptures on the façade, the kings
of Saint Trophime.

Don takes flash photos
of dark paintings and shows me.
I see them clearly.
We stumble into a courtyard
with a few glass offices.
Workers in ties look up.

We read the plaque
about the Deportation.
We see two small doors with iron grills.
Don's Jewish grandparents
emigrated from Rumania.
We must look Jewish,

though neither of us is,
I think, and feel we're "passing,"
all of this in my head
looking up again
at the well lit
offices across the courtyard.

We're mongrels,
each of us "creole"
in a sense and both of us
beyond the pale
together, and all this
unspeakably easy.

WATER AND LIGHT

From a high cliff, I watch a sailboat float
with a surfboard tethered to it carrying
a man paddling in his wetsuit safe
from the cold and wind. The sea's patched blue and green.
From my angle I can watch the keel
keeping the boat upright float with the whole
rocking in tandem.
                          A temperate wind
burnishes surfaces brighter than chrome.

I let myself be altered by this light
on water, calmed by how it changes, late
at night full moonlight glowing blackish green
on edges of the bright sheet, and at dusk
after a rain, the clouds still low, pastels,
ochres, echoing Cap Canaille, lying
over the water mirroring the layers,
the line of the horizon known only
by repeating parallel symmetries.
Along the bases of cliffs the slow waves strike,
swelling with sucking sounds, then receding
from gaps in limestone made by their striking,

needles and fissures, blow holes, angry bulls
charging somewhere from the mind's woods
distracted by the wine-red sea, the blood
of hearts spilt in a long, sad list of wars
staining the water some late afternoons
like this, and like an apparition, cliffs,
a face, King Chaos rising through the mirror.

LE CHEVAL BLANC

Gauguin

"It says the white horse but it's not
White it's green," says the young mother
To her son, holding his hand while

I lean against a pole in love
With the natural light that helps
Me see the light in the painting

Reflect in the water this horse
Bows to drink. His shaded flanks, too,
I think, flash with that cool light that

The fantastical bow tie bloom,
Periscope from oblivion,
Shares at water's edge near me (two

Lesser blooms like songbirds' chicks flick
Tongues, too, upward). Trees shade my right
At the stream's bank, light band of sand

Or gums, and someone stoops or bends
On a smaller dark horse into
And I think through trees that bow, too—

Then the stream—across which another
Horse, this one red, looks upward though
His rider's leaving the stream for

Sunlight and a meadow's yellow.
In the rocks everywhere I see
Lovely flesh, beloved flesh,

Pelvis, shoulders, and the hip's curve.
The horse Pegasus wears no wings
But this and the light water's kiss.

CARAVAGGIO'S *SAINT URSULA*

My flight is due to board in a few hours.
It will take me an hour, I calculate, once
I have left the exhibit, to buy my ticket,
catch the train, and reach the terminal so I
cut to the last room first because of the crowds
noticing in passing the Archangel's fierce eye
as he stands over Mary praying, head bent.

In another painting, Saint Ursula seems already
dead, though still conscious, almost green.
Her executioner has just let fly his arrow
at close range, and his well-dressed buddies
behind her, one in armor, don't even seem focused on what
has just happened. The old man's eyes seem wise
and yet untroubled. It's all very disorienting,
and I want to look behind me where they're looking
but despite myself follow Ursula's eye. The painter
has given the blur of the shaft as if both passing
and already passed and the first red gush
that I have had to stand still, and close, to see
in the crowd with the painter, no saint,
gasping as if struck through as he strikes.

LATE APRIL SNOW

The snow that fell all night
and much of the day
buried the fern's curl
toward light,

thickened the evergreens'
thin, airy branches.
Snow calls no sky down
and blanches

the world with bright,
diminished chances,
sighs the cold, mirror-
hard fire

till the sun laughs, harder.

BETWEEN BONNARD'S *L'ATELIER AU MIMOSA* AND *L'AUTO-PORTRAIT*

The high blues of the hills are licked
Gold, their red-topped fire flicked
On walls down the town's red tile roofs
Through four cattails
Leaning toward four blood rails
Leading out and in (what moves

Where's unclear) the acacia bright,
Painful, too hot, as if it might
Seer Eurydice back from the dead
(She's arched one brow
Incredulous—here, now—
A cool nimbus over her head,

Dead).
       Someone strolling stops to look,
His lover's neck in his arm's crook
Pulled in close as he licks his ear.
To "*que c'est beau
La vie*!" he adds this show
Flaming shamelessly near

The artist's bald, late self-portrait
Staring from his mirror straight
Through us, too, the steely gray
Gaunt head back lit
Still—soap, brush, toilet kit—
In this bath (rose-peach) of her day.

NOCTURNE

Frogs sing in trees with the night birds.
The lights go out and all the lights begin:
Low Mars burns red, and the orchards
          Bloom in moonlight
      (So white—they glow within),
And over walls, hedges, and the clay tiles
Of neighbors' roofs, the hills I see for miles.
         I think I might

Melt in this night and sky I see.
I met myself in Fontainebleau decades ago
Today climbing wedged in a stone chimney
         To throw myself
      Free at the top, though low,
Inching slowly so as not to slide down
Again through narrow wedged places I'd found
         To scale, a shelf

Safe enough to test to meet friends
Waiting for me below in the sand, above,
Lending a hand there where the slick stone ends—
         Boulders with scales
      On toe-holds—wedged, as if by love-
Spangled mica and whimsy to construct
This easy glee so, after all, I've lucked
         Out. The rest pales.

Three

LA VIERGE DE DOULEUR

by Germain Pilon, 1586
for Catherine of Medici

I can't help thinking when I look at you
About her who made him make you,
Her hands,

Virgin of Sadness, your hands crossed,
Head bowed, luminous marble
Shadowed with folds and pleats

Marrying light and shadow,
Your whole body flesh clothed
In flesh, organ-making (w)hole

Gland gathering goodness
In this round chapel with a narrow
Door in a dark locked church

Opened for once, with a guide
From whom I hide. I still
Catch a quick glimpse of you, Mother,

Your wrists crossed expressing
The son toward whom your
Face bends absent.

CAPITAL TOWERS

"I do not tell you these stories
so that you will feel sorrow
for my private losses,

but so you will understand
more and so be able
to make others understand."

Deng pauses. He and Agot address
the Coffee Club, on the top floor
of Capital Towers, overlooking

the Governor's mansion, Statehouse,
the decaying, grand
King Edward, and the Electric Building—

the last gutted like a fish,
its art deco scales intact and buffed
lustrous against brown marble.

My eye, intent ever
on artifice, wanders. I am a crow
with an eye for shiny things,

or am I like the decadent Roman
patron from Fellini's Petronius
who'd pay a poor man to let him

watch us have his
hand cut off? *You recoil?*
Well, so do I. But no,

no, this surely isn't why the gentleman
takes Agot's hand in both his and says,
"You've got quite a story. Thank you

for telling it to us." We mean
well, we all do mean well,
imagining ourselves or our families

wandering unprotected and wanting
more than anything
to be the protector, to stave

off harm. Brecht
hated tragedy because it gave
pleasure to an audience that instead

of *pathos* needed a new way
of seeing, not moving
endings or gutless facades. Change.

SALVATION

Young Dinka seminarians ask
Will God save the Muslims?
And those who sacrifice to gods—
The god of the spear, the god of the drum—
Or to the hungry ancestors?

Their teacher has been feeding them Tillich,
Barthes, and Daly, Thomas and Luther.
She cannot say,

"Finger not my treasure." (Herbert quipped
Through God's voice breaking the locks
Of the double covenant.)

When Ignorance forded the river quickly
To God, tinker Bunyan dispatched him
To Hell by infernal elevator.

When the people took Christ as their savior
The drum before which some
Left watches and little gifts
Of thanksgiving was burned to ashes.
"It was part of our heritage! It's lost forever!"
Lost, too, the fleet spear that traveled
From village to village.

Father Mark, "Father Elephant" in Dinka,
Wrote of his friendships with believers
Of the traditional religions.
Deprived of their talk, he felt diminished.
He did not deny their criticisms.

Deng's grandfather holds still to the old religion.
Once, he came home drunk.
Deng gave his grandfather a shower
And put him to bed. "My bad grandson
Baptized me! He made me a Christian!"
He would not be convinced or consoled.
His grandfather would not be taken
To a Christian heaven. That place
Would strip him of all the loving flesh
With which his spirit held communion.

STRASBOURG

The yellow and green rose, and the pink rock,
The chestnuts blooming, the cobblestone square,
Our Lady's tower rising everywhere,
Dark timbered fronts; the mechanical clock
Whose rooster crows three times for Peter's flock,
The Apostles, the old man's and the child's share
Of time—aspire I'd say to make me stare
And stop. I praise what I might otherwise mock,
The locked contingencies, the stock of losses,
Bright liquidity everywhere channeled,
A storied cityscape of destinies
Averted as when, turning, a young Turk tosses
His hands in the air and my chest's pummeled,
"My brother, forgive me!" and my thoughts freeze.

PROTECTION

The Security
Chief
seems always

angry. He wants
to protect me.
I'm not fair.

We're both angry.
He's right.
I won't stand

on my
merit. Degrees
are "academic."

He e-mails us all
on 9/11 Lincoln's
prayer

(1863)
when the blood
of sons

and fathers
was shed
for "national sins":

"Before the offended
Power,
to confess. . . ."

On the Sunday
after, Philip's our
crucifer. Towering

over us, he beams
to lead the processional. One
refugee says, "They

followed us here. We
brought this danger
to you," as if any guilt

felt whatever its
merit might answer
powerlessness.

COMMON WAYS

Little Gidding, Cambridgeshire

Near Saint John's Church, a ridge,
A Roman road, where people drove
Cattle to Cambridge market,
Pheasant roam the rows and roads.
Everywhere ancient common ways:
From Sawtry, through the fields, a path
(Across a field of yellow)
Still on a local map, with gates
That you might take and close.

Different bricks give evidence
Of age and order. Near the altar
Everything's oldest, and they brought
The altar itself down to stand
Among the people with the priest
Who faced them, to their north.

These were no Roman epicures.
Like them, though, set apart,
They left the state to its designs
And in a web of friendship held
Trembling, the fly of greed,
Mortifying the body's need,
Measuring their meat with weights,
"Watches," praying the psalms at night,
Nicholas sleeping on a board—

Medicine, bandages for the poor.
Poor boys who learned their Psalters earned
Pennies to spend or hoard.

Women with scissors bound and glued
Counter-Reformation prints
With Gospel passages to make
A book of "Harmonies."
Playing Socratic dialogues
They wrote in character
(In history they read
The hand of God in enemies
Rewarded for humility)
And musical interludes
In the Great Room, long since burned down,
Some "40 paces from the Church."

The King and court they fled
Came to them near the end.
Before Hampton Court or the trial
Charles sought solace here.

They passed their manuscripts with friends,
Susanna's found in George's hands
After he died. Nicholas, too,
Died early, his disease
Chronicled in letters as
Inscrutable as symptoms marked
By spots and agues, his despair
Doubled by the will's remorse.

Bathsheba thought them all rank mad
And fled after her husband's death
To London, on a wagon, in the hay,
John's brother Nicholas
In the end burning
The plays and poems of his youth.
The fires set the locals talking
Of witches, spells, and devils.

Prayer, valid everywhere,
By grace is the place
In which they rest and race.

In green April, I make my pilgrimage,
Smoke from refuse rising before
Prospects of hills and two spires,
The small pond winking through a copse,
Knee-high grass over the leaning stones,
Broken, illegible lines
Bowing to kiss their dust; inside—
An eagle (on which sits
The still Word) cleansed of the mire
Of the small pond, full centuries
Of water, lustrous brass again.
Talons on rock, the eagle lifts,
Resolute, stoic, in a sty
Where Mother Ferrar made their table,
The idol of iconoclasts
And heaven's honey, the heart's rest,
Exiled hope and wilderness.

PILGRIM

Near Travastere, I found (finally)
San Agostino, maps approximate
At best, names changing block by block, the feet,

The dirty soles, of Caravaggio's pilgrims
Who bowed to Mary, and the marble floor's
Polychrome under my feet shone near

The body of the martyr Benedict
And Monica, the mother of *Confessions*.
In Santa Maria in Travastere,

Mary is dead, and in the background
Christ held his mother childlike in his arms
But in a side niche, to the altar's left

Peter hung headlong not to mock his Lord's cross
With a crude look of confusion on his face
Or terror, the painter's execution crude

Power not Northern Gothic, startlingly
Small: its own kind. A chapel's cupola,
Elegant, Age of Reason, drew my eye

Up until standing beside Saint Joseph
Covered with butterflies, small folded notes
And Polaroids of people needing healing,

I felt as if I stood in Old New Spain,
The *Popagos'* (now *Tohono O'Odham*),
Lit candles in the Mission of San Luis,

A sixteenth-century wooden saint stretched out,
Recumbent agony with grief appended,
The pictured tubes and wires of old age

Or youth, two angels over the crossing
Dressed in white dresses, prayers at mass mixed with
The Moon and Sun and Wind, wild worldly forces

Whose spirits move and dance across the sky
As when, last night, my fireplace whined with force
Banging my shutters to get in. Before

I found the church of Saint Cecelia, who,
Beheaded patroness of music, lies
Silently white, face down, I walked through parts

Of Rome a little rougher, though still safe.
I felt safe, braced by a small town's distrust
Of the unknown. A wedding would take place

That afternoon. People were sweeping,
Unfolding carpets, setting up bouquets
Of flowers brightly arranged for the day

When I walked down into the crypt, my fee
In the palm of a sweet young African nun
In habit. Then, *oubliettes* like the hole

Villon was thrown down, but now I forget
Whether the Temple of Minerva led
Past the paste gems, the Roman home

Valerian knew, frescoes in the church
"like water after too much sweet," to quote
One patron. Now I'm getting all mixed up.

What did I see where? San Clemente's layers
—Familiar, incomplete—compete: Mithras,
The sun god, in a corner. Near the house

Still used when Emperor Constantine
Constructed a Creed and his new capitol,
I saw where you'd share meals in friendship

And bring a god to earth. An Irish guide
Planted his group. Looking to him, they blocked
The view inside. The house spring's gurgling still.

I ate a passable meal of lamb
Pasta with chicken at *Op!la!* that night
By myself. The waiter and I spoke French.

I made it an early night, watching the BBC's
World News report on indigenous cultures
And globalization. New roads cut old nets.

HOME

"*Agot*: the name means *Cobra*" (at the dinner table
after Dinka services, we're joking about names
and their meanings), though

actually it means more *this* (Agot, who will
study radiology, crooks his hand and wrist to imitate
the shape a cobra might make when standing

to strike). They have to pause and
translate this for me and Mary Ann, who's done
the cooking, since we've been wondering why they're

laughing so hard. (She raised a family of boys
she tells me, elbows on the table, smiling.)
I'll get it wrong, though. When they tell

stories, I usually remember
only the end and beginning: the man
who throws a spear at a monkey for the pure

fun of scaring the monkey, in the end
caught between a crocodile
and the vengeful monkey who has his own turn

at fun—or the father who, gorging himself
for the *fattest man competition* and who also simply
loves to eat, comes to a village festival

to be disappointed that it is mostly dancing
and courting and that the food after must be shared,
who eats an entire whale that has been stranded

on the river, having sent his gluttonous son
away on a wild goose chase so that he might
eat everything himself, which he does, *end*

of story. Laughter. Why do they tell these stories
after dancing for the first time in the nave of the church,
moving in a circle and leaping many feet

into the air? I have never seen them smile
so or glow, whirled by a distant center. (Reverend
Woja tells me that for a few minutes

they are all home again in Africa.) The Somali
Muslim woman they've brought with them seems
happy, too. (Abuk, who is with her, speaks Arabic.)

But I started all this talking about Agot
and cobras and food and got carried away.
Before the thirsty had plenty, Moses,

with the snake that had eaten Pharaoh's snakes,
stiffening again then into a staff, in Sinai
(Africa's ear), struck an improbable rock.

CROWN

"And God said, Let there be lights in the firmament of the heaven to divide the day from the night; and let them be for signs, and for seasons, and for days, and years"

—Gen. 1:14

ADVENT

How can the wolf not kill the lamb?
How can the rich be any less
Than in my heart I think I am?
What wars are won with gentleness?
How can the lamb trust and not die?
How can the poor be any more
Exalted by the King than I
Who clean his house and hold his door?
I'll take my sweet time, then, and make
My own hands' best work the place
That's safest, best, for my Lord's sake.
Faith's not an entrance singing grace.
So I, unbroken, still defy
His mild child till mute stones must cry.

CHRISTMAS

Visceral house, dark warmth, whose waters float
A sealed boat, ark of grace, containing all

Oceans inside you, through you the Word wrote
Us and you, who in your flesh bore light. Call
Dark night day, then, so sin, too, can sink
Buried with death, which these fresh waters drown
Better than years or ink. Blot out night, drink
Forgiveness; the child's hand, mouth, writes you down.
Unconquered Son, your church has made this day
That you made, from *Mithras, Sol Invictus,*
Elah-Gabal, not, though, from the same clay
We share or washed old hopes but a chaste rashness.
Eternity sleeps on the old year's bier
As the still word speaks so that we might hear.

ORDINARY TIME

Green season, wreath of Sundays, each a feast
Woven with years to lift new crowns of praise
Without delay, we leave the wise men east
Again, amazed, until we take highways
Of fire, confused to understand, schooldays,
His pupils teaching, foreigners come home,
That as we walk through his green wood's new maze
Again, we're set asea, and with Him, roam
Freely to find his ways our own and us
More ours in this, and his; his heart-sighs comb
Wheat with the sun's wind to make us lustrous.
We rise in his death, with his breath our compass.
We kneel to stand. We run. We discover
A life mysteriously familiar.

LENT

Tempered by hope, bright sadness, forty-day exile,
I fear I grow too happy in unhappiness,
Mastering myself (as if I could) through new denial
To set an idol up, false cross, and lose God's goodness.
Oh let me not, encumbered, stumble the long mile
Back the wrong way. And let my heart not love you less,
For this, sweet Jesus, that you antedate my trial
And my denial. (How could I take what you possess?)
You give your good gifts, and I lose all my merit.
How do I confess this last, worst, fear: your church sins,
And I in it. I wear Cain's mark and inherit
Silence, damnation's profit, and your old foe wins.
O God, forbid it! Must Death's laugh trump love's brilliance,
Rock of All Mirth, and the tomb swallow deliverance?

EASTER

Year's pivot, new day, here the whole year swings
Open forever through spring's first full moon,
Blood-stained posts, death's angel, and night's noon:
Christ's fire our door. Cut Isaac's fastenings!
Through the Red Sea, Egypt's slavery, God brings
His people home, so always now he will soon
Flower in orchards, bear his new fruit, and prune
The dead branches while risen Israel sings.
So that we might live truth, be our new life
That we might live; and living, give us joy

65

To live your peace, your joyous peace that gives
Joy to the stranger, joy that kills all strife
And pride, your joy that death cannot destroy,
Such joy your love, love's risen joy that lives.

WHITSUNDAY

New feast of weeks, new day of God's first fruits,
Heat, wind, and tongues: confusion rains down fire.
What can this mean? Nothing is as it seems.
You might as well tear up the tree by its roots
As mix us up like this! Call me a liar
Then, and set me on fire! I understand
Joel called what's true God's truth. Still, my worst dreams
Smile, calling me brother, and no one suits
Me like my own, though Peter's sights go higher.
David foresaw what this confusion means.
He is alive. Turned out, I think I meet,
Empty and hot, thirsty, and understood,
Him here in his city, turning to greet
Me freer than my own presumption would.

FEAST OF CHRIST THE KING

King of Glory, humiliation's crown,
Reigns from on high; the thief beside him sees
What others can't; and when they take him down,
Mary can see, not touch, God's mysteries,

And may I kneel, now, taste, and see what he
Gave to release me to freely return
Love as his gift in perfect liberty
Serving the King whose saints like near stars burn.
Diadems of his holiness and grace,
His living truth is justice, love, and peace,
A clear spring flowing from that holy place
Where laborers rest, knowing their release.
See, know, taste his goodness. He who was least
Offers himself in love, each day a feast.

HOLY CONVERSATION
Vittore Carpaccio

"The saints in conversation!"
She tells her husband across the small room
    Though alone myself I'd thought talk,
    The interchange of touch or look,
Or music's sound, or soundless print, the loom
        And shuttlecock's motion,

        The counterweighted bucket
Lifting more easily the well water
    For the hermit, his grotto cut
    In a skull's shape, might mean rather
I see my eye might thread the needle's eye
        Of the world and reply

        To arch on arch, lion
In his master's solitary labor
    Complicit, grateful, awaken
    To flimsy clay fording over
A clot of roots and trees beginning to leaf
        Over what's just enough

        Bridge to suffice and step
Across what's there in this picture, a boy
    With arms like water throwing seeds;—
    Then, that peak's eye: two black dots slap
A smaller third dot, infinity's toy,
        Which, where work fails, succeeds.

EMPLOYMENT

Why is a life not like a day?
The fruit trees flower. The clematis
      Opening a pink spray
Of gold centers like the wild rose
      Was made for this
Torrent of color. One lost bee
      Taps my windows
From inside before it flies free

Through blue the same bird welcomes
Each dawn's first fresh moments before
      Invisible flight comes
To me wondering where it's flown:
      From this near shore
To the boar's next hill—or the woods—
      Where some unknown
Spikes pierce through moss their paper hoods?

Bright mornings, cold useless use,
What good is there in this
      Urge I must feel to lose
My life in a fruitless push?
      A gold bomb's miss
Tripped in the tree in front of me
      Drops in a rush,
Wheels, white song's scythe, stone floor, grass sea.

COME OUT

Light sought me out, trimming the cumulous clouds
Over the spreading oak out my half-shaded window.
Come out, the clouds said, and I did.
I set my work down on the chair and went out
In the September air after a two-day rain.
The walls everywhere were transfigured.
Red apples hung unpicked across the way,
Archipelagos of clouds going golden,
Near the pier, the water
Shivering silver magenta,
A pink-bellied minnow spawning
Moving suddenly somewhere with great resolve
Setting red on the edges of the last dark blue clouds
Spreading spawn everywhere, vast sheets,
Before suddenly it shook and was gone.

SPRING

Wild violets
at my feet
I see
the birch
blister
white.

This
blue's
new.

A titmouse
trills and then
thunders
angrily
a thousand
wooden
mallets.

THE LOTUS TREE

January 15, 2005

As if swimming in a familiar river
from my youth, comforted and caressed
by a language moving me

as I call out or wave towards the shore,
I'm a young man with an ear again for all
the new thinking. Everything feels possible.

I walked from the train, past vineyards, their pruned
torsos, the rich earth
under them turned, perhaps, by these two men

in work boots (one in a floppy leather hat)
looking up. (Did they feel, like me, companionate
curiosity?) I turned: acacias blooming

little fits of gold, the hill's layered whites
and terra cottas at one with the town's stucco and tiles
till cliffs thrust abruptly into the sea

and sky as if to say, "See! See!
I'll take you with me!" (*Cap Canaille*—Cape
Scoundrel), the narrow

alleys winding past pharmacies and shops
past the white lighthouse quarried from stone
near Charlemagne's Crown (it has an emerald eye).

At its base men who'd walled
the sea lifted heavy bags of cement, passing
them down. "*Il n'y a pas de paradis*

terrestre." There is no heaven on earth
that lasts. The French name for the lotus tree
lulls like a dove's song. Homer wrote

that to eat its fruit was to lose all desire
to return home. Here, the *micocoulier* shades children.
They sing and run in the closed courtyard. Simon writes

through air to wish me well. My flight
here and the celebration at home
all took place on the same day, so I missed

Abuk's good food, the dancing in the nave, the smiles
after, and the quiet, hopeful prayers for peace:
a day like that finch, gold-breasted, in the highest branch.

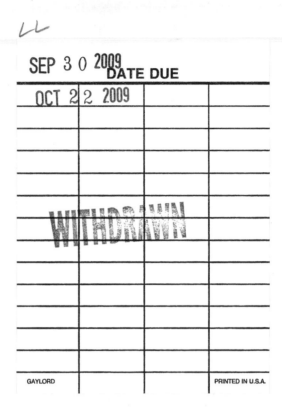